D1261316

A Closer Look at

Bacteria, Algae, and Protozoa

A Closer Look at
BACTERIA,
ALGAE, AND
PROTOZOA

Edited by Sherman Hollar

Britannica®
Educational Publishing
IN ASSOCIATION WITH

ROSEN
EDUCATIONAL SERVICES

Published in 2012 by Britannica Educational Publishing
(a trademark of Encyclopædia Britannica, Inc.)
in association with Rosen Educational Services, LLC
29 East 21st Street, New York, NY 10010.

Distributed exclusively by Rosen Educational Services.
For a listing of additional Britannica Educational Publishing titles, call toll free (800) 237-9932.

First Edition

Britannica Educational Publishing
Michael I. Levy: Executive Editor, Encyclopædia Britannica
J.E. Luebering: Director, Core Reference Group, Encyclopædia Britannica
Adam Augustyn: Assistant Manager, Encyclopædia Britannica

Anthony L. Green: Editor, Compton's by Britannica
Michael Anderson: Senior Editor, Compton's by Britannica
Sherman Hollar: Associate Editor, Compton's by Britannica

Marilyn L. Barton: Senior Coordinator, Production Control
Steven Bosco: Director, Editorial Technologies
Lisa S. Braucher: Senior Producer and Data Editor
Yvette Charboneau: Senior Copy Editor
Kathy Nakamura: Manager, Media Acquisition

Rosen Educational Services
Alexandra Hanson-Harding: Editor
Nelson Sá: Art Director
Cindy Reiman: Photography Manager
Matthew Cauli: Designer, Cover Design
Introduction by Alexandra Hanson-Harding

Library of Congress Cataloging-in-Publication Data

A closer look at bacteria, algae, and protozoa / edited by Sherman Hollar.
   p. cm. — (Introduction to biology)
"In association with Britannica Educational Publishing, Rosen Educational Services."
Includes bibliographical references and index.
ISBN 978-1-61530-534-6 ((library binding)
  1. Bacteria—Juvenile literature. 2. Algae—Juvenile literature. 3. Protozoa—Juvenile literature. I.
Hollar, Sherman.
QR74.8.C56 2012
579—dc23

2011012945

Manufactured in the United States of America

On the cover: Algae takes many forms. Seaweed, like the sample shown here, is one example.
Shutterstock.com

Interior background images Shutterstock.com

CONTENTS

In the 1700s, a Dutch draper made a startling discovery. Anthony van Leeuwenhoek had a passion for grinding glass into very precise magnifying lenses. He used these lenses to look close up at such things as the scrapings from his teeth. He wrote, "I then most always saw, with great wonder, that in the said matter there were many very little living animalcules (tiny animals), very prettily a-moving."

Leeuwenhoek became the first person to see and describe bacteria. Since that time, scientists have identified and classified thousands of minuscule living creatures. Three important categories of microorganisms— bacteria, algae, and protozoa—will be explored in this book.

Bacteria are prokaryotes. Prokaryotes don't have a real nucleus (the "brain" of a cell) the way a eukaryotic cell, such as that of an animal, has. Bacteria are much more primitive in design. But their simplicity also allows them to survive in many different environments. For instance, some bacteria need oxygen; some would be killed by it. Others, called facultative anaerobes, can live with or without it. *Salmonella*, one facultative anaerobe, can cause food poisoning.

Some bacteria are vitally important to life. Saprophytic bacteria, for instance, help organic matter rot and turn into rich fertile soil for growing new crops. Other bacteria turn milk into cheese and yogurt.

And yet, bacteria can also cause dangerous diseases. Some bacteria even create toxins that poison their victims, such as *Clostridium tetani*, which produces tetanus. Scientists have used bacteria to create bacterial antibodies to develop vaccines both to fight disease-causing bacteria and the toxins they produce.

Algae are eukaryotes (complex cells) that contain chlorophyll. This lets them make their own food through photosynthesis, but they are simpler than plants. Unlike bacteria, all of which are single-celled, algae can range in size. Many, such as dinoflagellates, are single-celled. Others are gigantic, such as the *Nereocystis luetkeana* kelp which can grow to be 115 feet (35 meters) tall. The word algae comes from a Greek word meaning seaweed, and indeed, seaweed is an important category of algae. But algae can also be found in freshwater, on rocks, and even on animals. Many algae are beneficial—for example, carrageenan, made from red algae, is often used

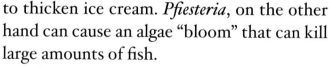

Women and children harvest and dry spirulina, *a blue green algae used as a dietary supplement, in Brandji, Chad, in 2009.* **AFP/Getty Images**

to thicken ice cream. *Pfiesteria*, on the other hand can cause an algae "bloom" that can kill large amounts of fish.

The word protozoa comes from the Greek words meaning "first animal." To get food, some of these eukaryotes can absorb

8

nutrients through their pellicle, or cell covering. Others devour their prey by surrounding them and entering them into special holes called vacuoles. In order to find food, many protozoa have special structures that allow them to move. Most commonly, they use cilia (short, hairlike extensions that work together in waves) or a flagellum (a long whiplike tail) to get around. Others, like the amoeba, move by the use of pseudopods (false feet). They simply let some of their watery fluid pour into one area of their body until it forms a long false leg that it can use to propel itself forward. While many protozoa are harmless, some are parasites, such as the genus *Plasmodium*, which causes malaria, a disease that kills two million people each year.

Leeuwenhoek and the many scientists who have discovered other bacteria, algae, and protozoa have done much to unlock one of the most mysterious domains of the world. Scientists today continue to make discoveries by trying to live up to the great lensmaker's motto: "By diligent labor one discovers matters that could not be discerned before."

CHAPTER 1

THE DIVERSE WORLD OF BACTERIA

The single-celled organisms called bacteria live on, in, and around most living and nonliving things. With few exceptions, bacteria can be seen only with the aid of a microscope, and millions of them would fit on the head of a pin.

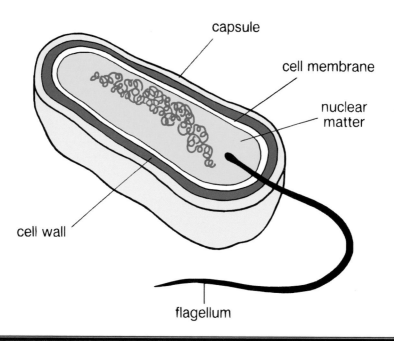

PARTS OF A GENERALIZED BACTERIAL CELL OF THE BACILLUS TYPE

capsule

cell membrane

nuclear matter

cell wall

flagellum

Parts of a bacterial cell. Encyclopædia Britannica, Inc.

Although some bacteria are harmful, many bacterial species are beneficial. Bacteria that live in the intestines of humans are essential in digesting food. Other species play a role in fermentation, a process that produces foods such as yogurt and cheese. Bacteria themselves are vulnerable to infection by viruses called bacteriophages.

The study of bacteria is called bacteriology. It often is integrated with studies of other microorganisms, or microbes, a diverse group that includes algae, archaea, fungi, and protozoa. These combined studies are called microbiology.

PHYSICAL CHARACTERISTICS OF BACTERIA

Bacteria are prokaryotes—that is, they have no distinct nucleus (sometimes called the "command center" of a cell) and they lack most of the internal structures found in the cells of more complex organisms called eukaryotes. Most biologists classify bacteria as constituting one of three domains of living organisms. Along with the domain Bacteria, these include the Archaea, which consists of prokaryotic organisms that have distinct molecular characteristics separating them

from bacteria, and the Eukarya, which consists of all other organisms, including plants and animals.

Scientists divide the bacteria into groups based on shape: spherical cells, which are labeled as cocci (sing., coccus); rod-shaped cells, called bacilli (bacillus); curved rods, known as vibrios; and spiral-shaped bacteria. The latter group is further divided into spirilla

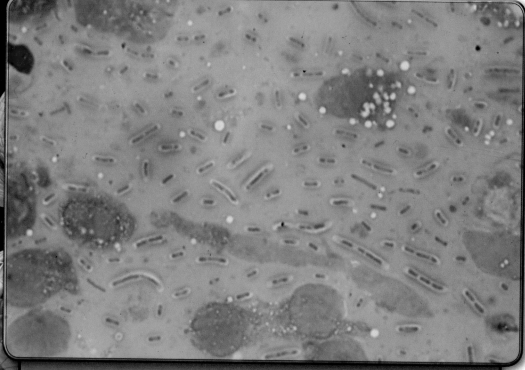

Bacilli, **Klebsiella pneumoniae,** *isolated from a lung abscess in a patient with pneumonia.* **A.W. Rakosy/EB Inc.**

(spirillum), which are rigid, thick spirals; and spirochetes, which are thin and flexible.

Virtually all bacteria have a cell wall surrounding a cell membrane. Within the cell membrane lies the cytoplasm, a jellylike substance composed of water, proteins, and other molecules. A single circular strand of DNA, a complex molecule that carries all the information about how a living thing will look and

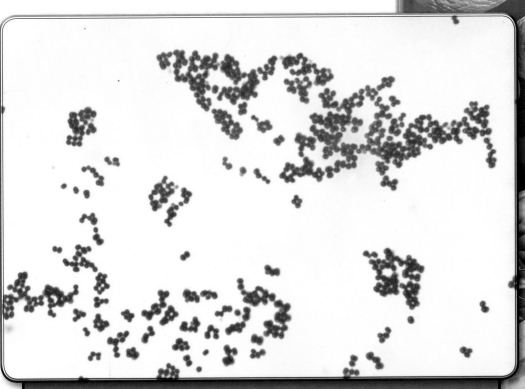

Cocci, **Staphylococcus aureus,** *in a laboratory culture.* **A.W. Rakosy/ EB Inc.**

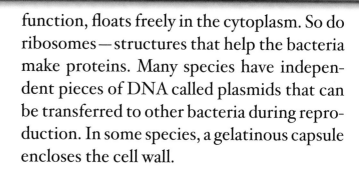

function, floats freely in the cytoplasm. So do ribosomes—structures that help the bacteria make proteins. Many species have independent pieces of DNA called plasmids that can be transferred to other bacteria during reproduction. In some species, a gelatinous capsule encloses the cell wall.

WHERE BACTERIA LIVE

Bacteria are found in a great variety of habitats. One teaspoon (5 milliliters) of fertile soil may contain as many as 500 million individual bacteria. Some species live on and within other living things, such as animals or fungi (a relationship known as symbiosis). Bacteria inhabit oceans, deserts, hot springs, and even snow.

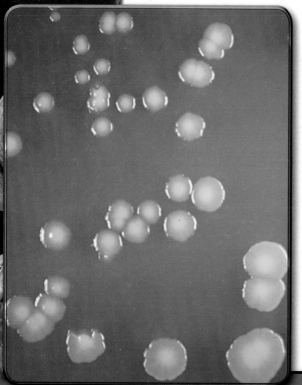

The bacteria Neisseria flava *from the human nasal passage.* A.W. Rakosy/EB Inc.

14

THE FIRST LIFE-FORMS

The earliest simple life-forms in the fossil record are prokaryotes—namely, bacteria and cyanobacteria (formerly called blue-green algae). They have been found in rocks called stromatolites, structures that are layered, globular, and often larger than a football

A submersible passes over stromatolites in the Caribbean in 2006. The mounds are composed of sticky mats of cyanobacteria that cement sand and sediments. Jonathan S. Blair/National Geographic Image Collection/Getty Images

and that generally contain calcium carbonate. Stromatolites formed when colonies of prokaryotes became trapped in sediments; they are easily identifiable fossils, obvious to a researcher in the field. Thin-sectioning of fossil stromatolites occasionally reveals the microscopic, fossilized cells of the organisms that made them.

Until about 2.5 to 2.8 billion years ago, the Earth's atmosphere was largely composed of carbon dioxide. Through photosynthesis—the process by which green plants and certain other organisms transform light energy into chemical energy—or related life processes, primitive bacteria and cyanobacteria captured large amounts of carbon and deposited it on the seafloor, removing the carbon from the atmosphere.

Through geologic processes, this carbon was carried into the Earth's crust. At present approximately 0.1 percent of the carbon fixed annually is lost to the biosphere in this way. During the Proterozoic (2.5 billion to 542 million years ago), this process allowed some free oxygen to exist in the atmosphere for the first time.

Cyanobacteria were also the first organisms to use water as a source of electrons and hydrogen in the photosynthetic process. Free oxygen was released as a result of this reaction and began to accumulate in the atmosphere, allowing oxygen-dependent life-forms to evolve.

They have been found high in the atmosphere, at the bottom of rivers and lakes, and in the deepest mines. Some species can survive the scorching temperatures of hydrothermal vents (a fissure in the ocean floor from which mineral-rich superheated water issues); polar-dwelling species are well adapted to subzero temperatures.

Columns of salt rising from the extremely saline waters of the Dead Sea. In this stressful environment, few life-forms other than bacteria can survive. **Peter Carmichael/ASPECT**

THE SIZE OF BACTERIA

Bacteria are generally smaller than the cells of eukaryotes, but larger than viruses. Bacteria are measured in units of length called micrometers, or microns. One millimeter is equal to 1,000 microns; it takes about 25,000 microns to make up one inch (2.5 centimeters). Some bacteria measure only one half a micron. In contrast, *Thiomargarita namibiensis*, a bacterium that lives buried in ocean sediment, can measure as much as 750 microns across (about 0.03 inch, or 0.75 millimeter), and can be seen without a microscope.

Most bacteria range from 1 to 5 microns in size. The light microscope can magnify an image approximately 1,000 times, and is used for basic studies of bacteria. Specialized microscopes, such as electron or phase-contrast microscopes, are used to examine special details of bacterial structure.

HOW BACTERIA LIVE

The diverse nature of bacteria becomes even more apparent when one considers how bacteria live. For example, bacteria can use almost any organic compound, and some inorganic compounds, as a food source. Some bacteria require oxygen, others do not, and some can live with or without it. Variations are also found with regard to bacterial loco-motion (or movement), spore formation, and reproduction.

NUTRITION

Bacteria absorb nutrients and secrete wastes through their cell walls. They secrete enzymes (substances that control how quickly chemi-cal reactions occur) that break down food in their immediate environment into soluble form so that it can pass through the wall and into the cytoplasm. Some bacteria can live on simple mineral compounds. Others have very complex food requirements. Autotrophic bacteria can manufacture organic nutrients— compounds such as carbohydrates, proteins, and vitamins—from simple inorganic sub-stances such as sulfur, water, and carbon dioxide from the air. Heterotrophic bacte-ria must obtain organic nutrients from their environment. This group includes patho-genic, or disease-causing, bacteria, which rely on their host to supply nutrients; and saprophytes, which live on decaying remains of other organisms.

RESPIRATION

Some bacteria species cannot tolerate exposure to oxygen. These bacteria are called anaerobes; they occupy a variety of habitats, such as soil and hot springs. Many are part of the normal bacterial life, or flora, that exist inside the gastrointestinal tract and mouth. *Treponema denticola*, which lives in dental

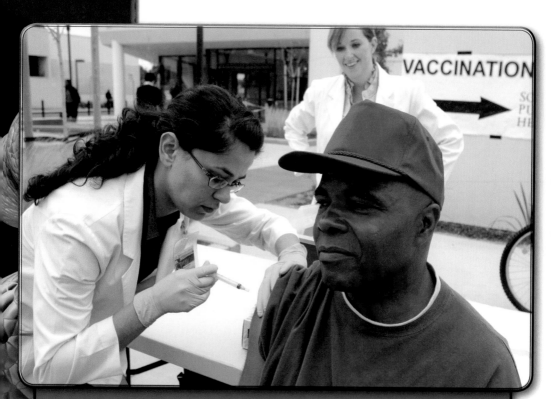

A medical student (left) administers a whooping cough vaccination on August 11, 2010, in Vallejo, California. The state was suffering its largest outbreak in more than fifty years. **Justin Sullivan/Getty Images**

plaque, is a good example. Bacteria that require oxygen are called aerobes. *Bordetella pertussis*, which causes whooping cough, is in this group.

Bacteria that can live with or without air are called facultative anaerobes. Some, such as *Escherichia coli*, are part of the normal body flora (although *E. coli* can also spread disease). Other facultative anaerobes, such as *Salmonella* and *Shigella*, are pathogenic.

LOCOMOTION

Many bacteria are able to move through liquids by means of taillike appendages called flagella, or tiny hairlike structures called cilia. Other species cannot move on their own, but are carried about on animals or insects, or through the air on dust.

SPORE FORMATION

Several groups of bacteria can form structures called endospores, or spores. The spore is a resting stage that enables the organism to endure adverse conditions. When conditions improve, the spores transform into active bacteria. Some spores, such as those that cause the diseases anthrax, botulism,

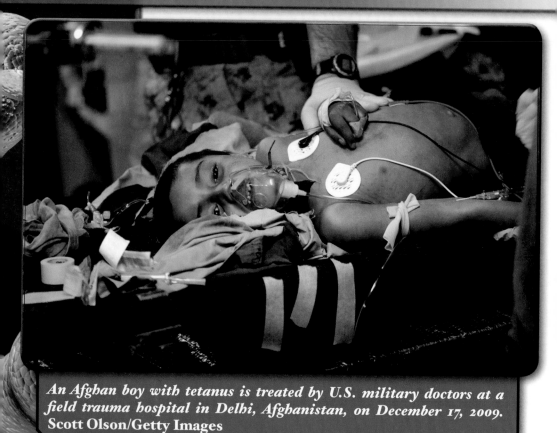

An Afghan boy with tetanus is treated by U.S. military doctors at a field trauma hospital in Delhi, Afghanistan, on December 17, 2009.
Scott Olson/Getty Images

and tetanus, can withstand extremely harsh conditions, including boiling water, extreme cold, and exposure to many chemical disinfectants, over long periods of time.

REPRODUCTION

Most bacteria reproduce asexually by dividing in two, a process called binary fission.

These two new cells grow and then each divides to form two new cells, resulting in a total of four cells with identical DNA from a single parent cell. Some species divide only every 16 hours or more. In the fastest growing bacteria, however, fission may occur as often as every 15 minutes, yielding billions of bacteria with identical DNA within 24 hours.

Some bacteria exchange genetic material before undergoing fission. In these species, a tubelike structure extends between two bacterial cells. The donor transfers portions of its DNA to the recipient. This allows bacteria to transmit certain genetic traits, such as drug resistance, to other bacteria in their population.

CHAPTER 2

THE IMPORTANCE, DANGERS, AND USES OF BACTERIA

It is impossible to overstate the importance of bacteria to the natural environment. Without bacteria, organic matter would not be broken down and soil would not be fertile. While some bacteria cause disease, scientists also use bacteria to create vaccines to fight infections. Moreover, researchers have found a variety of ways in which bacteria may be utilized in food production, agriculture, and industry.

SIGNIFICANCE IN NATURE

The decomposition of organic material (substances that contain carbon) in nature is brought about chiefly by vast numbers of saprophytic bacteria, though saprophytic fungi contribute to the process. If there were no decay, the remains of dead organisms and the waste of cities would accumulate so fast that they would soon

interfere with everyday life. As saprophytes break down organic matter, such as rotting leaves and dead insects, they enrich the soil by returning minerals and nutrients to it. A by-product of the decomposition is carbon dioxide, which is used by plants in photosynthesis.

Although plants need nitrogen to grow, plants cannot use nitrogen gas, which is abundant in the air. Several kinds of bacteria can take nitrogen from the atmosphere and convert it into a form that is usable by plants, a process called nitrogen fixation. Some nitrogen-fixing bacteria, such as *Rhizobium*, occupy nodules on roots of legumes (plants such as peas and beans) and live in a mutualistic, or mutually beneficial, relationship with the plants. Other nitrogen-fixing soil bacteria, such as *Azotobacter*, are free living and release fixed nitrogen into the soil, where it can then be taken up by a plant's roots.

HOW BACTERIA CAUSE DISEASE

Pathogenic bacteria may enter the body in many ways, such as through the mouth or through cuts in the skin. If they multiply

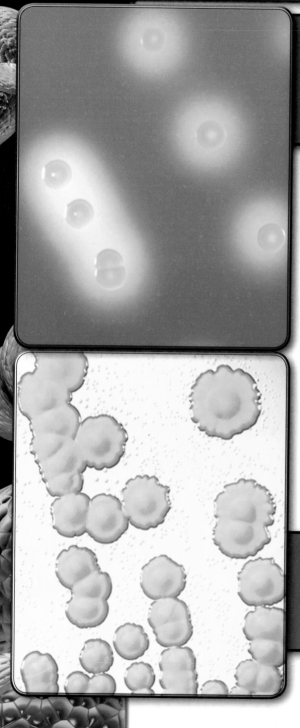

Typical bacteria from infections include beta-hemolytic streptococci, *from the sore throat of a child who later developed rheumatic fever.* A.W. Rakosy/EB Inc.

sufficiently they can cause an infection. The infection may be caused by the microbes themselves, or by poisons called toxins that they produce. Some toxins, such as those produced by *Staphylococcus aureus*, are more dangerous than the bacteria. Plants, too, are vulnerable to bacterial infections, though they are plagued by different species than are animals.

Typical bacteria from infections include Hemophilus influenzae, *isolated from a child suffering from spinal meningitis.* A.W. Rakosy/ EB Inc.

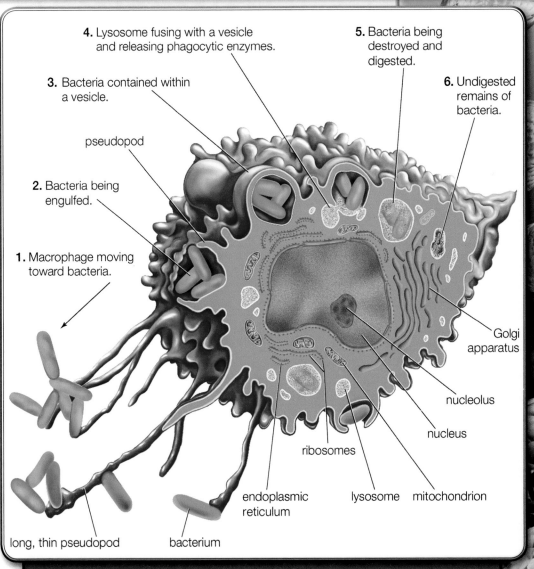

4. Lysosome fusing with a vesicle and releasing phagocytic enzymes.

5. Bacteria being destroyed and digested.

3. Bacteria contained within a vesicle.

6. Undigested remains of bacteria.

pseudopod

2. Bacteria being engulfed.

1. Macrophage moving toward bacteria.

Golgi apparatus

nucleolus

nucleus

ribosomes

long, thin pseudopod

bacterium

endoplasmic reticulum

lysosome

mitochondrion

Macrophages, the principal phagocytic (cell-engulfing) components of the immune system, ingest and destroy foreign particles such as bacteria. **Manfred Kage/Peter Arnold, Inc., (bottom) Encyclopædia Britannica**

TYPES OF BACTERIA THAT CAUSE DISEASE IN HUMANS

BACTERIA	PRIMARY DISEASES IN HUMANS
Bacillus anthracis	anthrax
Bacteroides species	abscess
Bordetella pertussis	whooping cough
Borrelia burgdorferi	Lyme disease
Campylobacter species	campylobacter enteritis
Chlamydia species	psittacosis; trachoma; lympho-granuloma venereum; conjunctivitis; respiratory infection
Clostridium species	botulism; tetanus; gangrene
Corynebacterium diphtheriae	diphtheria
Escherichia coli	gastroenteritis; urinary tract infection; neonatal meningitis
Gardnerella species	vaginitis; vulvitis
Haemophilus influenzae	meningitis; bacteremia; pneumonia
Helicobacter pylori	peptic ulcer
Klebsiella pneumoniae	pneumonia
Legionella species	Legionnaire disease; Pontiac fever
Moraxella lacunta	conjunctivitis
Mycobacterium species	tuberculosis; leprosy

BACTERIA	PRIMARY DISEASES IN HUMANS
Mycoplasma pneumoniae	fatal pneumonia
Neisseria gonorrhoeae	gonorrhea; gonococcal conjunctivitis
Pasteurella species	pasteurellosis
Pseudomonas aeruginosa	nosocomial infections (infections acquired in a hospital setting); gastroenteritis; dermatitis; bacteremia; pericondritis (ear disease)
Rickettsia species	Rocky Mountain spotted fever; boutonneuse fever; typhus; trench fever; scrub typhus
Salmonella species	salmonellosis (e.g., food poisoning or typhoid fever)
Shigella species	shigellosis (dysentery)
Staphylococcus aureus	wound infection; boils; food poisoning; mastitis
Streptococcus pyogenes	rheumatic fever; impetigo; scarlet fever; puerperal fever; strep throat; necrotizing fasciitis
Treponema pallidum	syphilis
Vibrio cholerae	cholera
Yersinia enterocolitica	yersiniosis
Yersinia pestis	plague

The Dangers of *E. coli*

Escherichia coli bacteria normally inhabit the stomach and intestines. When *E. coli* is consumed in contaminated water, milk, or food or is transmitted through the bite of a fly or other insect, it can cause gastrointestinal illness. Mutations can lead to strains that cause

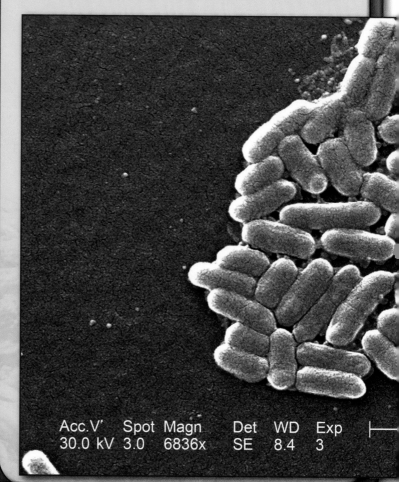

Acc.V' Spot Magn   Det WD   Exp
30.0 kV 3.0   6836x   SE   8.4 3

diarrhea by giving off toxins, invading the intestinal lining, or sticking to the intestinal wall. Therapy for gastrointestinal illness consists largely of fluid replacement, though specific drugs are effective in some cases. The illness is usually self-limiting, with no evidence of long-lasting effects. However, one dangerous strain causes bloody diarrhea, kidney failure, and death in extreme cases. Proper cooking of meat and washing of produce can prevent infection from contaminated food sources. *E. coli* also can cause urinary tract infections in women.

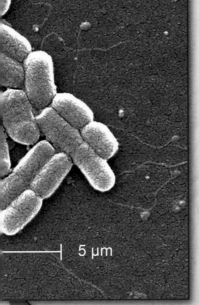

5 μm

Colorized scanning electron micrograph showing a number of Escherichia coli *bacteria.* Janice Haney Carr/CDC

VACCINES, ANTITOXINS, AND ANTIBIOTICS

Vaccines can be produced that protect humans and animals from infections by certain pathogenic bacteria and their toxins. Vaccines against bacterial infection are typically prepared by using killed or weakened specimens of the pathogenic bacteria dissolved in a solution. When injected into the body the material stimulates the individual's immune system to form antibodies against the microbe, thus protecting the individual from becoming ill if infected in the future.

Antitoxin injections contain preformed antibodies. They are prepared by injecting bacterial toxins into live animals. The blood is later collected and the serum is separated from it by chemical means. Antitoxins act more quickly than vaccines, but the protection usually lasts no more than a few weeks or months. Vaccines, however, protect for a year or longer.

Some kinds of microorganisms secrete substances called antibiotics that can destroy other microbes. Penicillin, the best-known antibiotic, is the product of a mold. Bacitracin and polymyxin are made by bacteria. Many widely used antibiotics, such as

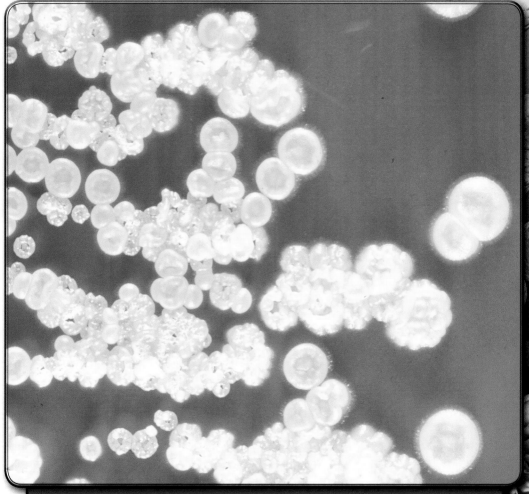

Colonies of **Streptomyces griseus** *were isolated from soil.* **A.W. Rakosy/EB Inc.**

streptomycin, neomycin, erythromycin, and tetracycline, come from members of the genus *Streptomyces*, a group of soil bacteria with mold-like characteristics.

THE DISCOVERY OF PENICILLIN

Penicillin was discovered in September 1928. It has saved millions of lives by stopping the growth of the bacteria that are responsible for blood poisoning and many other once fatal diseases. This miracle drug was discovered and given to the world by Alexander Fleming, a physician and research bacteriologist at St. Mary's Hospital Medical School in London.

In World War I Fleming served as a medical captain, specializing in the study and treatment of wounds. He was deeply impressed by the high death rate from bacterial infection of wounds. His discovery of penicillin greatly reduced the death rate from wounds in World War II.

Fleming was studying deadly bacteria in 1928 when he made his dramatic discovery. Always retiring and modest, he attributed it to "the greatest fortune." However, it was fortune combined with a gift for scientific observation and a genius for research.

For examination purposes Fleming had removed the cover of the bacteria culture plate with which he was working. A mold formed on the exposed culture. A less gifted scientist would have thrown away the accidentally contaminated culture. Fleming, however, noticed that in the area surrounding the mold, the bacteria had disappeared.

Penicillium notatum, *the source of penicillin.* Carlo Bevilacqua— SCALA/Art Resource, New York

He kept a strain of the mold alive and began testing it on laboratory animals. In 1929 he published his first medical paper proving that a lowly mold from soil was a powerful microbe killer that did not injure human tissue.

For years chemists were unable to extract enough pure concentrated penicillin to use in medicine. Fleming kept his mold, but the world of science almost forgot it. Then in 1938 a team of Oxford University scientists, headed by Howard Florey and Ernst B. Chain, remembered the research paper of nine years earlier. World War II interfered with the large-scale manufacture of penicillin in Great Britain. But methods for its mass production, purification, and stabilization were developed in the United States. In 1945 Fleming shared the Nobel prize for physiology or medicine with Florey and Chain.

Bacteria in Foods

The bacteria that bring about decay are the chief cause of food spoilage. For fresh foods, the decay process may be slowed down by refrigeration or checked by freezing. When frozen food is thawed, however, the bacteria become active again.

Many kinds of bacteria can be killed by heat. Because few species grow in foods that are acidic, dried, salted, or very sweet, it is easier to process foods with these qualities. For example, canning acidic foods such as tomatoes is less complicated than processing green beans. The amount of heat required to can nonacidic foods successfully is very high because of the need to destroy thermophilic (heat-loving) bacteria and their spores.

As some bacteria and other microbes "digest" nutrients, they produce certain chemical products through a process called fermentation. Dairy products are fermented in many ways to produce products such as sour cream, buttermilk, cheese, and yogurt. Cheeses owe their various flavors almost entirely to different kinds of combinations of bacteria and mold.

BACTERIA IN INDUSTRY, MEDICINE, AND AGRICULTURE

Fermentation is also important to the chemical industry. Because they can be grown quickly and in vast quantities, bacterial cells are used as miniature chemical factories, producing a wide range of substances— some of which can only be produced by bacteria. The solvents butyl alcohol (used in lacquers) and acetone are formed by *Clostridium* bacteria. A *Lactobacillus* species makes lactic acid from corn starch or whey. *Acetobacter* uses alcohol to synthesize acetic acid, the ingredient that gives vinegar its characteristic flavor. Dextran, which is used to expand blood volume in cases of hemorrhage or dehydration, is made by a *Leuconostoc* bacterium from sucrose, common table sugar.

Certain bacteria are able to consume or break down pollutants or toxic materials in the environment, an application called bioremediation. Such bacteria are sometimes used, for example, to remove petroleum that pollutes the water after an oil spill. In the late 20th century scientists discovered a way to transfer genes from plants

and animals into certain bacterial cells. As the bacteria multiplied, they produced the product coded for by the transferred gene. The technology is used to produce a variety of substances, including insulin and human growth hormone, and has many applications in fields ranging from medicine to agriculture.

SOME COMPOUNDS PRODUCED BY BACTERIA ON AN INDUSTRIAL SCALE		
PRODUCT	BACTERIUM	APPLICATION OR SUBSTRATE
amylases	*thermophilic Bacillus species*	used in brewing to break down amyloses to maltoses
cellulases	*Clostridium thermocellus*	release of sugars from cellulose in waste from agriculture and papermaking
proteases (thermolysin, subtilisin, aqualysin)	*Thermus aquaticus Bacillus species*	used in brewing, baking, cheese processing, removal of hair from hides in the leather industry, and laundering

PRODUCT	BACTERIUM	APPLICATION OR SUBSTRATE
glucose isomerase	*Bacillus coagulans*	conversion of glucose to fructose as a sweetener in the food industry
beta-galactosidase	*Thermus aquaticus*	hydrolysis of lactose in milk whey to glucose and galactose
cobalamin (cyanocobalamin)	*Pseudomonas stutzeri*	
vinegar	*Acetobacter species*	from alcohol
monosodium glutamate	*Micrococcus species*	from sugar
dextran	*Leuconostoc mesenteroides*	from sucrose

BACTERIA IN THE LABORATORY

In the laboratory, bacteria are grown in a substance called a culture medium. Liquid media in test tubes is used for many types of bacterial research. In other studies, a solidifying agent such as agar (obtained from seaweed) is added to the mixture, which is poured into a shallow plate called a petri dish and allowed to congeal. Bacteria are applied

to the surface of the jellylike medium, where they grow and form patches called colonies, each containing millions of individual bacterial cells.

The nutrients added to the cultures depend on the species' requirements. Autotrophic bacteria can grow on powdered

Bacteria that produce color include Pseudomonas aeruginosa, *from sputum.* A.W. Rakosy/EB Inc.

sulfur and other inorganic substances and get carbon from carbon dioxide in the air. Sugars, amino acids, and vitamins are used for some heterotrophs. Blood may be added to cultures used to grow some pathogenic species. The identification of bacteria can be difficult and traditionally requires application of numerous

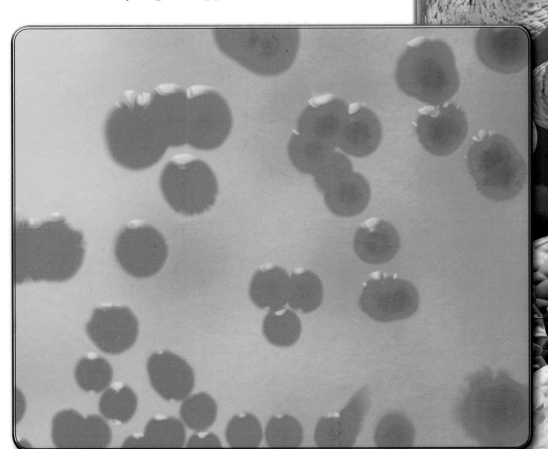

Bacteria that produce color include **Serratia marcescens,** *from a dirty utensil.* **A.W. Rakosy/EB Inc.**

criteria, including microscopic observations of the size, shape, and appearance of the bacteria after they have been stained.

THE DEVELOPMENT OF BACTERIOLOGY

Bacteriology is the branch of microbiology dealing with the study of bacteria. The beginnings of bacteriology paralleled the development of the microscope. The first person to see microorganisms was probably the Dutch naturalist Anthony van Leeuwenhoek, who in 1683 described some animalcules, as they were then called, in water, saliva, and other substances. These had been seen with a simple lens magnifying about 100–150 diameters. The organisms seem to correspond with some of the very large forms of bacteria as now recognized.

As late as the mid-19th century, bacteria were known only to a few experts and in a few forms as curiosities of the microscope, chiefly interesting for their minuteness and ability to move. Modern understanding of the forms of bacteria dates from Ferdinand Cohn's brilliant classifications, the chief results of which were published at various periods between 1853 and 1872.

LOUIS PASTEUR AND THE GERM THEORY

In 1854 French chemist and microbiologist Louis Pasteur became professor of chemistry and dean of the school of science (Faculté des Sciences) at the University of Lille. Hearing of Pasteur's scientific ability, a local distiller came to him for help in controlling the process of making alcohol by fermenting beet sugar. Pasteur saw that fermentation was not a simple chemical reaction but took place only in the presence of living organisms. He learned that fermentation, putrefaction, infection, and souring are caused by germs, or microbes—organisms too small to be seen except through a microscope.

Pasteur published his first paper on the formation of lactic acid and its function in souring milk in 1857. Further studies developed the valuable technique of pasteurization. The same year he was appointed manager and director of scientific studies at the school where he had received his doctor of science degree, the École Normale Supérieure. During the next several years he extended his studies into the germ theory. He spent much time attempting to convince doubting scientists that germs do not originate spontaneously in matter but enter from the outside. Microorganisms were finally recognized as a cause of disease in 1876, when

German bacteriologist Robert Koch proved that a bacterium was the cause of the disease anthrax. The germ theory's acceptance led to improved health practices, methods of food production, sanitation, and antiseptic surgical methods, and to the practices of quarantine and immunization.

Other researchers, such as Louis Pasteur and Robert Koch, established the connections between bacteria and the processes of fermentation and disease. Important discoveries came in 1880 and 1881, when Pasteur succeeded in immunizing animals against two diseases caused by bacteria. His research led to a study of disease prevention and the treatment of disease by vaccines and other agents. Other scientists recognized the importance of bacteria in agriculture and the dairy industry.

Bacteriological study subsequently developed a number of specializations, among which are agricultural, or soil, bacteriology; clinical diagnostic bacteriology; industrial bacteriology; marine bacteriology; public-health bacteriology; and sanitary, or hygienic, bacteriology.

CHAPTER 3

FEATURES AND TYPES OF ALGAE

Algae consists of a large variety of organisms, from those that appear as a green stain on damp rocks and tree trunks to those that form a fine scum on quiet ponds and the massive seaweeds that float in the ocean. In general, algae are organisms that are made up of one or more eukaryotic cells (cells with a true nucleus) that contain chlorophyll and that are less complex than plants. Many types of algae consist of single cells. Others types can form colonies or filaments of cells or, as in kelp, simple tissues. Approximately 27,000 marine and freshwater species of algae have been described.

Algae are found all over the Earth, particularly in oceans, rivers, lakes, streams, ponds, and marshes. They sometimes accumulate on the sides of glass aquariums. Although usually found in water and moist places, some species of algae inhabit the soil and can survive dry conditions for a long time. Algae may be found on leaves, especially in the tropics and subtropics, and on wood and stones. Some

species live within or on plants and animals. Certain species capable of tolerating temperatures of 176 °F (80 °C) dwell in and around hot springs, and certain other species live in the snow and ice of the Arctic and Antarctic regions.

Marine algae, such as the common seaweeds, are most noticeable on rocky coastlines. In northern temperate climes they form an almost continuous film over the rocks. In the tropics they are found on the floors of lagoons, and they are associated with coral reefs and island atolls. There are several species of algae that contribute to reef formation by secreting calcium carbonate. In Arctic and Antarctic waters they extend to considerable depths. In fresh water, the algae growth may be greatly increased by nutrient-rich pollution, such as a runoff that contains fertilizer.

As a group, the algae are not easily defined. For many years algae were categorized as plants because of their ability to carry out photosynthesis. Later, the algae were placed within the diverse kingdom Protista (a group

Edible algae being dried on a beach near Hisanohama in Fukushima ken (prefecture), Japan. **W.H. Hodge**

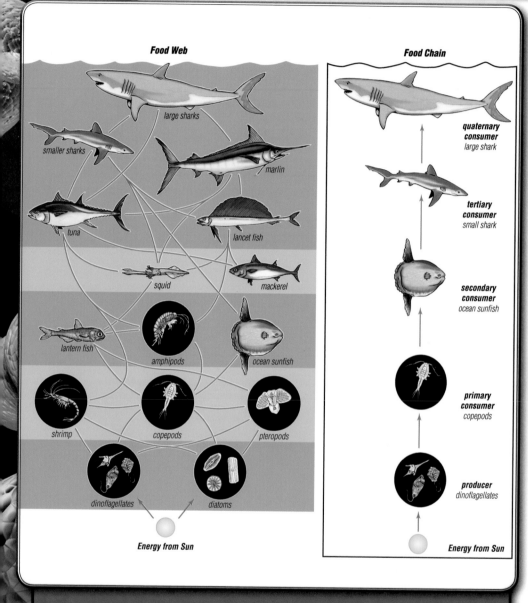

Algae, primarily diatoms, dinoflagellates, and coccolithophorids, which are often collectively called phytoplankton, are the base of the food chain for all marine organisms. Encyclopædia Britannica, Inc.

of eukaryotic, predominantly single-celled microscopic organisms). Despite this classification, the major groups of algae do not share a close evolutionary relationship. Algae play many roles—sometimes beneficial and sometimes harmful, depending upon the species—in the biology of organisms around them. In the natural world, algae are the chief food source for many fish and other aquatic organisms, and they contribute substantially to the store of oxygen on Earth.

Characteristics of Algae

The word algae comes from the Latin word for seaweeds. *Algae* is the plural form of the word *alga*, which denotes a single algal organism. Algae species range in size and composition from the tiny single-celled *Micromonas* to the giant multicellular sea kelps that aggregate into the underwater kelp forests found along continental coastlines. The sea kelp *Nereocystis luetkeana* may grow up to 115 feet (35 meters) in length, while *Micromonas* measures under three microns—the size of a large bacterium—and is visible only under a microscope.

Most algae, regardless of their external color, contain the green pigment chlorophyll.

This substance makes it possible for these algae to use the energy of sunlight to manufacture their own food (carbohydrates) out of carbon dioxide and water via the process of photosynthesis. Other pigments also are present, giving the different algae the distinct colors that are used as a basis of classification.

The study of certain types of algae lends insight into the evolution of plants. Such study has shown that green algae and plants are closely related and thus share an evolutionary history. Green algae and plants share many characteristics, including the composition of their chlorophyll pigments and their cell walls. Although green algae have no true roots, stems, or leaves, these traits are also characteristic of the Bryophyta, a group of plants that includes mosses and liverworts.

The simplest algae are single-celled organisms that float about in the water and absorb food through their cell walls. They multiply asexually by various methods, including fission (simple cell division) and a method called budding, in which one cell grows out

Green algae covering rocks along the Pacific coast in Oregon. © **liquidlibrary/Jupiterimages**

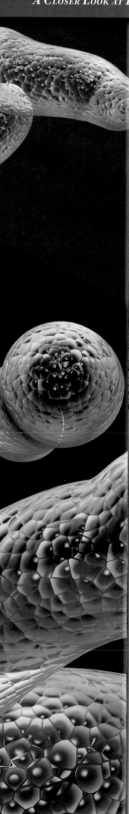

from another. Among the larger algae, methods of reproduction vary greatly. Sometimes a small section breaks away from the main plant to grow into another complete new plant. This is called fragmentation. Budding cells may remain clinging to the parent cells. Sometimes they bud all around the sides and form mats or long chains of cells called filaments. Some of these filaments and mats float onto rocks in quiet places where the motion of the water is not strong enough to carry them off again. These filaments cling to the surface while the floating cells wave in the water, gather the food, bud, and spread into feathery, leaflike fronds. The portion that clings to the rocks or other substrate is called a holdfast.

Some species of multicellular algae reproduce by means of spores—tiny collections of reproductive tissue that form on the alga's surface and are washed away by the water. When the spores ripen, they are washed off. These free-floating bodies then develop into adult cells. A number of the larger algae species can undergo sexual reproduction. These species produce tiny reproductive bodies called gametes, which are released into the water. There, the gametes combine with gametes of the opposite sex to form a new alga.

MAIN CATEGORIES OF ALGAE

Multicellular algae are commonly categorized into three main groups: the green algae, or Chlorophyta (from the Greek words *chlor*, meaning "green," and *phyt*, meaning "plant"); the brown algae, or Phaeophyta (a name based on the Greek root *phaeo*, meaning "dusky," or "dark"); and the red algae, or Rhodophyta (a name derived from the Greek word *rhod*, meaning "rose," or "red").

Most of the red and brown algae are marine species, though there are some rare freshwater species in each group. Green algae tend to be freshwater inhabitants, though there are some marine species.

Commonly recognized groups of largely single-celled algae include the golden algae, or Chrysophyta (from the Greek word for "golden plant"), and the dinoflagellates. Most species of golden algae live in fresh water, whereas most species of dinoflagellates live in marine environments. A third important group of single-celled algae, the diatoms, are closely related to golden algae.

As was mentioned early, blue-green algae make up another group of single-celled organisms that use photosynthesis to create food. However, because they do not have

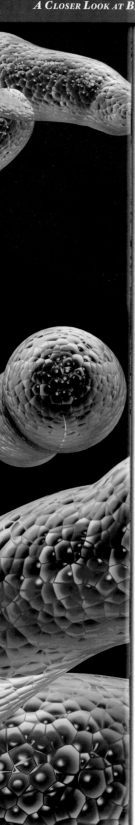

eukaryotic cells, they are not classified as algae but as a type of chlorophyll-containing bacteria called cyanobacteria.

Rhodophyta: The Red Algae

Many of the most beautiful plants on the seashore are red algae. There are roughly 5,200–6,000 species of algae in this group, which is called Rhodophyta. The majority of red algae live in tropical marine habitats, and most species are multicellular. Red algae have a complex life history, which means they go through several stages of development as independent organisms in order to complete their life cycle. Most undergo sexual reproduction.

Like many algae, rhodophytes contain chlorophyll and thus are able to photosynthesize their own food. Red algae also contain the reddish pigment phycoerythrin, which confers on them their characteristic color. Because of its light-absorbing properties, this pigment enables red algae to live deep beneath the water surface.

A number of species of red algae, such as laver, dulse, and Irish moss, are harvested for food. Laver (any member of the genus *Porphyra*) is the source of nori, dried thin sheets of seaweed popular in Japanese cuisine. Agar and carrageenan, gelatinous substances found in the cell walls of several species of red algae, are important for a variety of commercial applications, including use as a thickening agent in ice cream and other dairy products.

PHAEOPHYTA: THE BROWN ALGAE

This group of algae includes roughly 1,500 species worldwide. Most brown algae are marine, and they are found in cold temperate waters. Species of *Fucus*, or rockweed, live in the intertidal zones of rocky shorelines. There are also some tropical species, such as the free-floating masses of *Sargassum*. All phaeophytes are multicellular and range in size from seaweed made up of filaments, such as the species *Ectocarpus*, to the giant kelp that form underwater forests. Among the largest of the kelp are members of the genera *Laminaria*, *Macrocystis*, and *Nerocystis*.

Brown algae are so colored because of the presence of a brown pigment called fucoxanthin. Because the amount of this pigment can vary from species to species, phaeophyte species range in color from olive green to dark brown. Brown algae may undergo asexual or

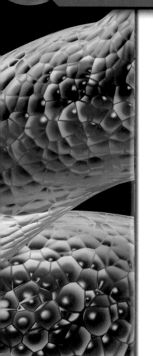

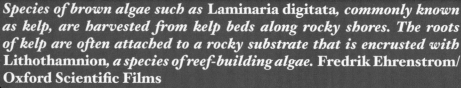

Species of brown algae such as **Laminaria digitata**, *commonly known as kelp, are harvested from kelp beds along rocky shores. The roots of kelp are often attached to a rocky substrate that is encrusted with* **Lithothamnion,** *a species of reef-building algae.* **Fredrik Ehrenstrom/ Oxford Scientific Films**

sexual reproduction. The spores and gametes produced, respectively, have two flagella of unequal length.

The phaeophytes are an important source of algin, a substance used in food processing and other industries. Certain species of brown algae are also used as fertilizer, and several, such as species of *Laminaria*, are eaten as a vegetable in Asia.

THE SARGASSO SEA

A free-floating meadow of seaweed almost as large as a continent lies between the United States and Africa in the North Atlantic Ocean. This is the famous Sargasso Sea. Christopher Columbus discovered it as he sailed toward the New World in 1492. Its presence suggested that land was near and encouraged him to continue.

The tangled seaweed of the Sargasso Sea is brown marine algae belonging to the genus *Sargassum*, popularly called gulfweed. Most of the weeds are *S. natans*, a free-floating species, but many other species of *Sargassum* grow attached to rocks along coasts. *S. natans*, which is kept afloat by its small but prominent berrylike air bladders, travels with the wind and current. It supports a specialized marine life and provides for seabirds a resting place in the middle of the ocean.

An inch-long baby flying fish swims in berried branches of sargassum, Sargasso Sea, Atlantic Ocean. Paul Zahl/ National Geographic Image Collection/Getty Images

Chlorophyta: The Green Algae

There are approximately 6,000–8,000 species in this group, 10 percent of which are marine. Some are free-floating, but most live on shore rocks or in large aggregations on stagnant water, such as in ponds. Several species are terrestrial and are found growing on trees and rocks in moist habitats.

The presence of chlorophyll is self-evident in the coloration of green algae. However, the

Halimeda discoidea *is a green algae.* Douglas P. Wilson

presence of other pigments may affect the coloring of some species, so that in fact, individual species of green algae range in color from yellowish-green to very dark, almost blackish-green.

Some species of green algae reproduce asexually, usually by simple fission or fragmentation; however, some species release spores. Sexual reproduction is more common, however.

The green algae Ulva lactuca, *commonly known as sea lettuce, is easily harvested when it is exposed at low tide. Many people living in coastal societies consume sea lettuce in salads and soups.* **Alison Wilson**

Green algae are a vital link in the food chain that supports living things on Earth. They serve as a direct food source for many aquatic organisms and are an important source of oxygen, which is produced as an end-product of photosynthesis. Some species, such as *Ulva*, or sea lettuce, are consumed by humans.

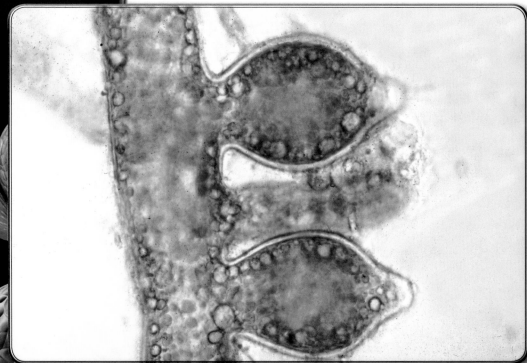

A species of yellow-green alga called Vaucheria sessilis *is an example of a sexually reproducing alga. The reproductive structures consist of an antheridium, which contains male gametes (sex cells), and two oogonia, which contain female gametes.* **Robert W. Hoshaw/EB Inc.**

However, green algae can also pose problems. Under certain environmental conditions, they may undergo rapid and uncontrolled reproduction. This results in a "bloom" that covers lakes and ponds, blocking light from reaching the lower depths. This sets off a chain of events: the decreased light causes a drop in photosynthesis, which leads to dramatically reduced oxygen production. Many organisms such as fish and zooplankton that live in the deeper zones of the water are dependent on the oxygen produced from the photosynthesis of algae and aquatic plants. But when photosynthetic rates drop and oxygen production ceases, these organisms die.

CHRYSOPHYTA: THE GOLDEN ALGAE

The members of the division Chrysophyta are fairly diverse. Although some chrysophytes are found in marine habitats, the majority of the roughly 1,000 species in this group are found in cold freshwater environments. The chrysophytes are generally single-celled flagellates—organisms that have a whiplike appendage called a flagellum. Their golden color comes from the presence of the secondary pigment fucoxanthin.

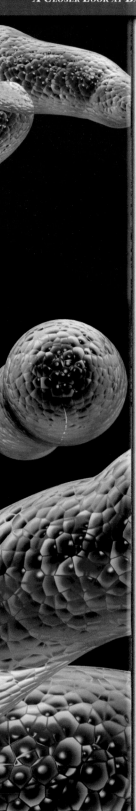

Not all members of the Chrysophyta are completely autotrophic (make their own food). Many members of this group are facultative heterotrophs. This means that under certain conditions—such as the absence of light or the presence of abundant readily available nutrients in the water— they behave as heterotrophs (organisms that consume other organisms for food). Such a life strategy is an adaptation that allows the organisms to survive under a wide variety of circumstances.

Sexual reproduction among the chrysophytes is rare. Most species reproduce asexually by the formation of spores or by simple fission.

The Diatoms

The diatoms are single-celled photosynthetic organisms covered with a tiny shell or exterior skeleton rich in silicon. They exist in very large numbers in the ocean and in bodies of fresh water. When diatoms shed their shells, the shells fall to the bottom and can form deposits that may build up to several meters. Diatomaceous earth—sedimentary rock formed from such deposits—has a number of commercial applications, including use in filters, insulation, and abrasives.

THE DINOFLAGELLATES

As a group, the dinoflagellates are sometimes called Pyrrophyta, a name derived from the Greek words for "fire plants." The name refers to the fact that some species of dinoflagellates are capable of bioluminescence, a

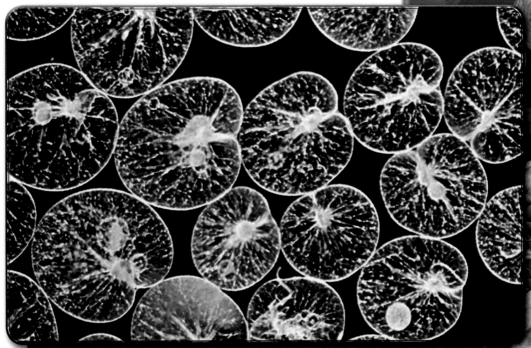

A species of dinoflagellate known as Noctiluca scintillans, *commonly called sea sparkle, is a type of algae that can aggregate into an algal bloom, producing substances that are potentially toxic to marine life.* **Douglas P. Wilson**

phenomenon in which certain chemicals in the organism undergo a reaction and produce light. Bioluminescence is found among other aquatic organisms as well. Experts estimate that there are roughly 2,000 species of dinoflagellates, most of which are marine. The freshwater species inhabit a wide variety of environments, and some even live in snow.

The dinoflagellates are exceedingly diverse. Some dinoflagellates use photosynthesis to create their own food—and are therefore autotrophic—and others are heterotrophs. Some species may exist as phytoplankton (free-floating autotrophs), while others may live inside other organisms, such as sponges or jellyfish, in a symbiotic relationship. Like the diatoms, photosynthetic dinoflagellates are extremely important sources of nutrients for larger organisms in aquatic environments.

Under certain conditions, such as warm water temperatures and increased nutrients, dinoflagellate populations can explode, or bloom. When this happens, the organisms create the serious environmental problem known as a red tide—so named because the enormous increase in the density of organisms causes the water to appear reddish.

RED TIDES

Red tides occur when coastal waters become overpopulated with certain types of algae and phytoplankton, including dinoflagellates, a type of single-celled algae. Many of the plankton species associated with red tides produce potent toxins that pose a serious threat to fisheries, marine ecosystems, wildlife, and human health. Once found primarily in the coastal waters of the United States and Europe, red tides have become a global problem.

Red tide, Tampa Bay, Florida, showing fish kill and red coloration caused by dinoflagellates. R.F. Head—The National Audubon Society Collection/Photo Researchers

The term red tide originated because some dinoflagellates contain reddish pigments. When these species reach high concentrations, the water appears to be colored red. The scientific community generally uses the term harmful algal bloom or HAB, when referring to outbreaks of algae that have adverse effects. The blooms are not associated with tides, and may have gotten that name because the blooms are frequently found close to shore.

The chain of events that cause HABs is uncertain. Scientists speculate that pollution may play a role in the blooms that originate near shorelines in shallow water. Many pollutants, such as phosphates, add nutrients to the water at a rapid rate, disturbing the natural dynamics of the ecosystem and leading to conditions that favor the growth of the dinoflagellates at the expense of other organisms. The algae colonize the area and outcompete native species, resulting in a bloom. *Pfiesteria* is an example of an organism that thrives in polluted water. It is associated with many significant fish kills from the middle Atlantic states to Florida.

Certain species pose a severe threat to the health of marine life and humans alike because they produce toxins that cause paralysis and death.

CHAPTER 4

FEATURES AND TYPES OF PROTOZOA

Protozoa, or protozoans, are single-celled microorganisms. Unlike bacteria and archaea, protozoa are eukaryotic. This means that they have a distinct nucleus. Also, unlike single-celled algae, protozoa cannot make their own food, so they eat other organisms. For this reason, protozoa were once considered animals. The term protozoan comes from Greek words *protos*, meaning "first," and *zoion*, meaning "animal." Protozoa make up a variety of groups of organisms within the kingdom Protista, though these groups do not necessarily share a common evolutionary history.

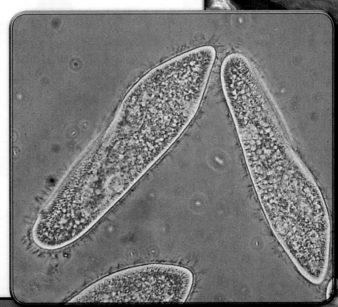

Paramecium caudatum *is an example of a protist.* John J. Lee

67

CHARACTERISTICS OF PROTOZOA

Most protozoa are too small to be seen without the aid of a microscope. Their shapes vary, but all protozoa have several features in common: a nucleus or several nuclei; mitochondria, bodies that perform special metabolic functions (the process of converting food to energy on a cellular level); vacuoles, which perform a number of functions, including digestion and

Shafiqa, 14, waits for treatment at a clinic for leishmaniasis in 2010 in Kabul, Afghanistan. This disease, caused by a protozoan parasite, can lead to severe scarring, often on the face. **Paula Bronstein/Getty Images**

water elimination; and other particles and organelles.

Protozoa occur widely in nature, particularly in aquatic environments. Because they thrive on moisture, protozoa are found in moist soil, fresh water, and oceans. Some exist as parasites inside the bodies of larger animals. Certain parasitic protozoa cause disease in humans and other animals.

Each protozoan is a complete living unit. It feeds, excretes, grows, and reproduces. Many protozoa have special structures that help them move. Protozoa traditionally have been classified according to differences in method of locomotion, number of nuclei, type of organelles (tiny organs inside a cell), life cycle, and mode of reproduction.

TYPES OF PROTOZOA

Ciliated protozoa, or ciliates, are characterized by a covering of short, hairlike structures called cilia. The cilia move in wavelike patterns and are used like oars to propel the organisms and to help direct food particles into their mouths. Ciliates have cell membranes, or walls. The cytoplasm, or cell material, of these protozoa is dotted with small pouches called vacuoles. Some

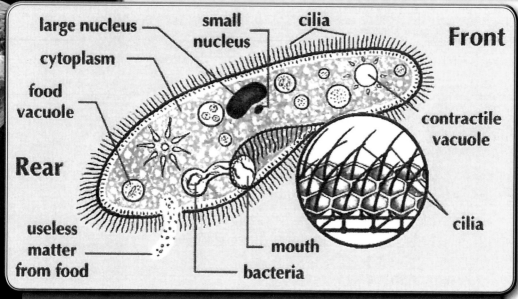

large nucleus

small nucleus

cilia

Front

cytoplasm

food vacuole

contractile vacuole

Rear

cilia

useless matter from food

mouth

bacteria

The paramecium swims freely in its search for food such as bacteria. It captures the prey with its cilia (also shown enlarged). Enzymes in the food vacuoles digest the prey, and contractile vacuoles expel excess water. **Encyclopædia Britannica, Inc.**

vacuoles digest food and other vacuoles expel water. The latter contract to squeeze out water and are therefore called contractile vacuoles. The paramecium is perhaps the most commonly known example of the ciliates. The basic shape of a paramecium varies, depending on the species: for example, *Paramecium caudatum* is elongated and gracefully streamlined and *P. bursaria* resembles a footprint.

Children nap under a mosquito net in 2010 in Prey Mong Kol, Cambodia. These nets, which contain a mosquito-killing insecticide, help prevent the insects from infecting people with malaria-causing protozoa. **Paula Bronstein/Getty Images**

Apicomplexans represent another type of protozoa. Unlike ciliates, all apicomplexans are parasites which move passively and anchor themselves firmly inside the organism they invade. They feed by absorbing fluids, such as blood, from the animal in which they live. The parasite that causes malaria is the apicomplexan *Plasmodium*. This protozoan,

Plasmodium: Malaria-Causing Parasites

Malaria is a serious relapsing infection caused by protozoa of the genus *Plasmodium*. These parasitic microorganisms are transmitted by the bite of the female *Anopheles* mosquito.

Known since before the 5th century BC, malaria occurs in tropical and subtropical regions near swamps. The roles of the mosquito and the parasite were proved in the early 20th century. Annual cases worldwide are estimated at 250 million and deaths at 2 million. Malaria from different *Plasmodium* species differs in severity, mortality, and geographic distribution. The parasites have an extremely complex life cycle; in one stage they develop at the same time inside red blood cells. Their mass fissions at 48- or 72-hour intervals cause attacks lasting 4–10 hours. Shaking and chills are followed by fever of up to 105 °F (40.6 °C), with severe headache and then profuse sweating as temperature returns to normal. Patients often have anemia, spleen enlargement, and general weakness. Complications can be fatal. Malaria is diagnosed by detecting the parasites in blood. Quinine was long used to alleviate the fevers. Synthetic drugs, such as chloroquine, destroy the parasites in blood cells, but many strains are now resistant. Malaria prevention requires preventing mosquito bites: eliminating mosquito breeding places and using insecticides or natural predators, window screens, netting, and insect repellent.

which infects red blood cells in birds and reptiles as well as in mammals, occurs worldwide, especially in tropical and temperate zones.

Flagellated protozoa, or flagellates, are organisms that possess—at some time in their life cycle—one flagellum to many flagella for movement and sensation. A flagellum is a hairlike structure capable of whiplike lashing movements. (Although flagella are somewhat similar to cilia, they are considerably larger.) Many flagellates have a thin, firm pellicle (outer covering) or a coating of a jellylike substance. Reproduction is either asexual or sexual. Flagellates may be solitary, live in colonies, free-living, or parasitic. Parasitic forms live in the intestine or bloodstream of the host. Sleeping sickness, also called African trypanosomiasis, is caused by the flagellate protozoan *Trypanosoma brucei gambiense* or the closely related subspecies *T. brucei rhodesiense*, both of which are transmitted by the tsetse fly.

Protozoa known as sarcodines are characterized by their ability to move through the use of temporary structures called pseudopods, or "false feet." A thin, flexible membrane surrounds sarcodines and contains their almost-liquid mass. It is easy, therefore, for parts of this mass to flow.

Amoebas: Nature's Efficient Blobs

A tiny blob of colorless jelly with a dark speck inside it—this is what an amoeba looks like when seen through a microscope. The colorless jelly is cytoplasm, and the dark speck is the nucleus. Together they make up a single cell of protoplasm. Amoebas are usually considered among the lowest and most primitive forms of life. But simple as they may seem, these tiny one-celled organisms carry out their activities competently and efficiently.

The amoeba has two kinds of cytoplasm: at the surface, a stiff, gellike cytoplasm forms a semisolid layer that acts as a membrane. It holds the inner, more watery cytoplasm and its contents together. The membrane is flexible, taking on the shape of the more watery cytoplasm inside, which is continually moving and changing the body shape of the amoeba. The name amoeba comes from a Greek word that means "change."

It is by changing its body shape that the amoeba travels. First it extends a lobelike pseudopod, then slowly pours the rest of its body into the pseudopod, which enlarges and finally becomes the whole body. New pseudopods form as old ones disappear. Their shapes range from broad and blunt to long, thin, sometimes branching structures. Often many pseudopods form at the same time in an uncoordinated way, as though the amoeba were starting off in all directions at once. But most pseudopods exist only for a short time, then flow back into the main body.

The amoeba feeds mainly on other microscopic, one-celled organisms such as algae and bacteria, as well as other tiny protozoa that live in the surrounding water. The amoeba has no mouth or other body parts for taking in or digesting food. If it finds itself near something edible, it may put out pseudopods to surround the food and flow over it. In this way, the food,

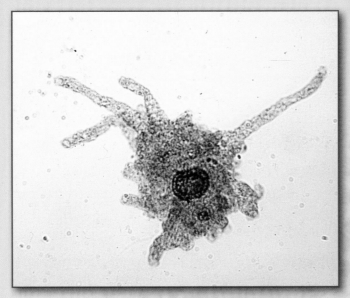

Fingerlike extensions from the amoeba's single cell are called pseudopods, or false feet. Fluid cytoplasm forms and flows into these everchanging lobes, enabling the protozoan to move. **Russ Kinne/Photo Researchers**

along with a tiny drop of water around it, is completely enclosed in a bubblelike chamber in the amoeba's body. The chamber is called a food vacuole, and an amoeba may have several in its body at the same time. Once the food is digested, the vacuole disappears.

If an amoeba is cut apart, it instantly forms a new membrane over the cut surfaces. The part containing the nucleus may survive, but the other part cannot digest food and eventually dies.

The nucleus is necessary for reproduction, which is asexual. The nucleus simply pinches in two in the middle; the two halves pull apart; each takes half the cytoplasm; and one amoeba has become two. The process, called fission, takes less than one hour.

When the protozoan is stimulated to move, a fingerlike projection oozes from its body. This is the pseudopod. The remainder of the organism flows into the extending pseudopod. Sarcodines may be either solitary or live in colonies. Although some are parasitic on plants or animals, most sarcodines are free-living, feeding on bacteria, algae, other protozoa, or organic debris. The most commonly known member of this group is the amoeba.

CONCLUSION

As this volume has illustrated, our lives are interwoven inextricably with microorganisms such as bacteria, algae, and protozoa. Microbes abound in the soil, in the seas, and in the air, and many species may be found on and within the human body. Although they usually go unnoticed, microorganisms provide ample evidence of their presence—sometimes unfavorably, as when they produce toxins and cause diseases, and sometimes favorably, as when they play their roles in the fertility of soils. With regard to Earth's ecology, in fact, microorganisms are of incalculable value, disintegrating animal and plant remains and converting them to simpler substances that can be recycled in other organisms. Of course, they are also useful in many other ways—for example, in the production of various foods, chemicals, and antibiotics.

Because microbes are relatively easy for researchers to work with, they provide a simple vehicle for studying the complex

processes of life. They have become a powerful tool for studies in genetics and of vital activities at the molecular level. This intensive probing into the functions of microbes is ongoing and has resulted in numerous and often unexpected dividends, including the means of controlling many diseases and infections.

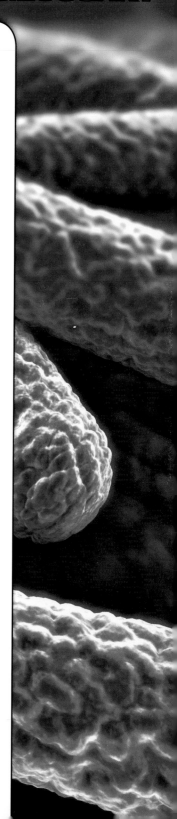

alga Any plant (such as seaweed) of a group that forms the lowest division of the plant kingdom and includes forms mostly growing in water, lacking a system of vessels for carrying fluids, and often having chlorophyll masked by brown or red coloring matter.

antibody A substance produced by the body that combines with an antigen and counteracts its effects or those of the microscopic plant or animal on which the antigen occurs.

antitoxin Any of various specific antibodies that are formed in response to a foreign and usually poisonous substance introduced into the body and that can often be produced in lower animals for use in treating human diseases by injection.

archaea Any of a group of single-celled prokaryotic organisms that have distinct molecular characteristics separating them from bacteria as well as from eukaryotes.

binary fission Reproduction of a cell by division into two approximately equal parts.

bioluminescence The emission of light from living organisms.

chlorophyll Any member of the most important class of pigments involved in photosynthesis.

cilia Tiny hairlike structures of many cells that make lashing movements.

cytoplasm The protoplasm of a plant or animal cell except for the nucleus.

eukaryote Any organism composed of one or more cells, each of which contains a clearly defined nucleus enclosed by a membrane, along with organelles.

fermentation Chemical breaking down of an organic substance (as in the souring of milk or the formation of alcohol from sugar) produced by an enzyme and often accompanied by the formation of a gas.

fissure A narrow opening or crack.

flagellum A long whiplike structure by which some tiny plants and animals move.

fungus Any of a major group of flowerless plants, such as molds, rusts, mildews, smuts, and mushrooms, that lack chlorophyll and are parasitic or live on dead or decaying organic matter.

gamete A mature sex cell that usually has half of the normal number of chromosomes and is capable of uniting with a gamete of the opposite sex to begin the formation of a new individual.

heterotroph An organism that relies on an organic source of carbon, originated as part of another living organism, and is unable to produce organic substances from inorganic ones.

photosynthesis The process by which green plants and certain other organisms transform light energy into chemical energy.

prokaryote Any of the typically unicellular microorganisms that lack a distinct nucleus and membrane-bound organelles.

protozoan Any of a phylum or group of tiny, animal-like organisms that are not divided into cells and have varied structure and physiology and often complicated life cycles.

pseudopod An outward extension of part of a cell that is produced by the pressure of moving cytoplasm (as in an amoeba) and that helps to move the cell and to take in its food.

ribosome One of numerous small RNA-containing particles in a cell that are sites of protein synthesis.

saprophyte An organism that lives on the dead or decaying material of plants and animals.

vacuole A cavity in bodily tissues or in the protoplasm of a single cell that is usually filled with fluid.

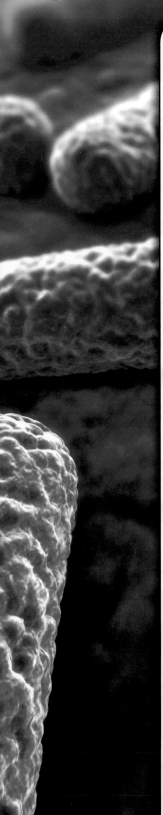

American Institute of Biological Sciences (AIBS)
1900 Campus Commons Drive
Suite 200
Reston, VA 20191
(703) 674-2500
Web site: http://www.aibs.org
Committed to advancing research and education in all aspects of the biological sciences, AIBS creates a number of programs and resources for students and the public at large, such as its ActionBioscience.org Web site.

American Society for Microbiology (ASM)
1752 N Street NW
Washington, DC 20036-2904
(202) 737-3600
Web site: http://www.asm.org
The central organization of microbiologists in the United States, the ASM provides information and resources for students interested in microbiology as well as professionals in the field.

Botanical Society of America (BSA)
4475 Castleman Avenue
St. Louis, MO 63110
(314) 577-9566

Web site: http://www.botany.org
The members of the BSA consist of professionals, academics, and educators who seek to share their research interests and promote the study of plants and related organisms with the public through the BSA's publications and outreach programs.

Canadian Society of Microbiologists (CSM)
17 Dossetter Way
Ottawa, ON K1G 4S3
Canada
(613) 482-2654
Web site: http://www.csm-scm.org
The members of the CSM consist of professionals, academics, and students dedicated to sharing their research interests in the field of microbiology and promoting interest in the subject among the public.

Laboratory for Algae Research and
    Biotechnology (LARB)
Arizona State University
College of Technology and Innovation
Department of Applied Sciences and
    Mathematics
7231 E. Sonoran Arroyo Mall, ISTB III,
    Room 203
Mesa, AZ 85212

(480) 727-1410

Web site: http://larb.asu.edu

LARB is dedicated to the study of algae and
discovering its uses in such processes as the
production of renewable energy and the
development of pharmaceuticals.

National Microbiology Laboratory (NML)
Public Health Agency of Canada (PHAC)
1015 Arlington Street
Winnipeg, MB R3E 3R2
Canada
(204) 789-2000

Web site: http://www.nml-lnm.gc.ca

As part of the PHAC, the NML is committed to the study and control of infectious
disease in Canada.

WEB SITES

Due to the changing nature of Internet links,
Rosen Educational Services has developed an
online list of Web sites related to the subject
of this book. This site is updated regularly.
Please use this link to access the list:

http://www.rosenlinks.com/biol/lvth

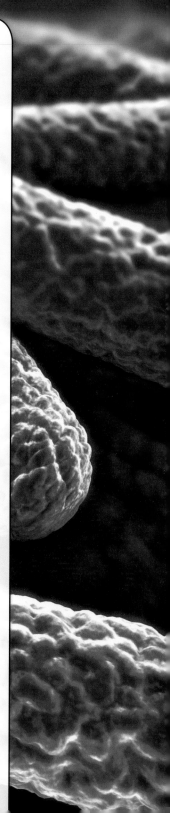

Farrell, Jeanette. *Invisible Allies: Microbes That Shape Our Lives* (Farrar, Straus, and Giroux, 2005).

Favor, Lesli J. *Bacteria* (Rosen, 2004).

Graham, Linda E., and Wilcox, Lee Warren. *Algae*, 2nd. ed. (Benjamin Cummings, 2009).

Guilfoile, Patrick, and Alcamo, I. Edward. *Antibiotic-resistant Bacteria* (Chelsea House, 2007).

Latta, Sara L., and Kunkel, Dennis. *The Good, the Bad, the Slimy: The Secret Life of Microbes* (Enslow, 2006).

May, Suellen. *Invasive Microbes* (Chelsea House, 2007).

Parker, Steve. *Protozoans, Algae & Other Protists* (Compass Point Books, 2010).

Pascoe, Elaine. *Single-celled Organisms* (PowerKids Press, 2003).

Snedden, Robert. *The Benefits of Bacteria* (Heinemann Library, 2000).

Wearing, Judy. *Bacteria: Staph, Strep, Clostridium, and Other Bacteria* (Crabtree, 2010).

INDEX

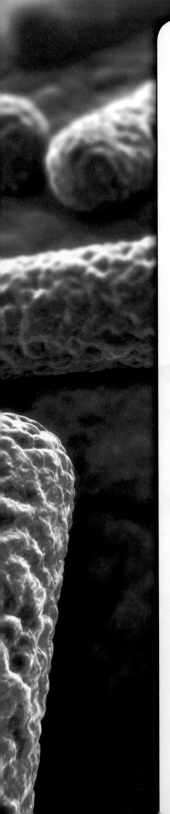